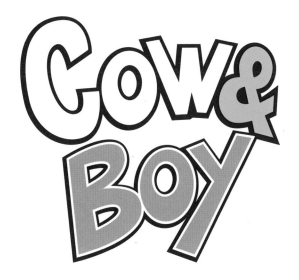

by Mark Leiknes

Andrews McMeel
Publishing, LLC
Kansas City

Cow & Boy is distributed internationally by United Feature Syndicate.

Cow & Boy copyright © 2008 by Mark Leiknes. All rights reserved. Printed in Singapore. No part of this book may be used or reproduced in any manner whatsoever without written permission except in the case of reprints in the context of reviews. For information, write Andrews McMeel Publishing, LLC, an Andrews McMeel Universal company, 4520 Main Street, Kansas City, Missouri 64111.

08 09 10 11 12 TWP 10 9 8 7 6 5 4 3 2 1

ISBN-13: 978-0-7407-7098-2
ISBN-10: 0-7407-7098-5

Library of Congress Control Number: 2007937787

www.andrewsmcmeel.com

ATTENTION: SCHOOLS AND BUSINESSES

Andrews McMeel books are available at quantity discounts with bulk purchase for educational, business, or sales promotional use. For information, please write to: Special Sales Department, Andrews McMeel Publishing, LLC, 4520 Main Street, Kansas City, Missouri 64111.

For Lisa

Introduction

Thank you for buying the first *Cow & Boy* collection. This book is especially meaningful to me because I remember immersing myself in my favorite comic collections growing up. Sure it was fun to visit "my friends" for a minute each day in the newspaper, but there was always something special about picking up a book and spending an entire afternoon with them.

Enjoy,

Mark Leiknes
November 2007

THE STRANGER RODE INTO TOWN ON HIS TRUSTY STEED...

CLOP, CLOP

...AND **DANGER** FOLLOWED. YES, EVERYONE KNEW RIGHT AWAY THAT LIFE WOULD NEVER BE THE SAME AGAIN....

CLOP, CLOP

...AND WHY AM I ALWAYS THE **STUPID HORSE**?

BUT YOU'RE THE NARRATOR, TOO.

WHOOPTY DOO.

WEEEE!!

HEE-HEE HEE-HA-HA!!

FASTER!! FASTER!!

WOULD IT KILL YOU TO PEDAL?

CLUMP CLUMP

YOU KNOW IN SOME CULTURES THE COW IS HELD **SACRED**.

OH YEAH, WHY'S THAT?

IT'S BECAUSE WE...

CAN GRANT WISHES?

ER, NO...

ARE GOOD AT MATH?

NO...

CAN WRITE POETRY?

NO...

CAN MAKE PUDDING?

NO...

ARE MADE OF BUNNIES?

NO...

KNOW KUNG FU?

YES, IT'S CUZ WE KNOW KUNG FU.

ROCKIN'!

KEEYAH!!

CRAKK

HMMM.

HMMMMM.

HMMMMM MMMMM MMMM.

SO, I JUST GOT BEAT BY A COW.

I WASN'T GOING TO SAY ANYTHING.

WOW, SO THIS IS WHAT IT FEELS LIKE TO BE A GIANT.

ACTUALLY GIANTISM IS A DISORDER OF THE PITUITARY GLAND THAT CAUSES A PERSON TO GROW ABOVE AND BEYOND WHAT SOCIETY CONSIDERS NORMAL.

AS A RESULT, EVERY TIME SOMEONE WITH GIANTISM WALKS INTO A ROOM THERE ARE ALWAYS RUDE ONLOOKERS WHO POINT OR DRAW ATTENTION TO A FRAGILE HUMAN BEING WHO ONLY EVER WANTED ONE THING OUT OF LIFE... AND THAT WAS TO BLEND IN.

WOW, SO THIS IS WHAT IT FEELS LIKE TO JUST STAND ON A FENCE POST FOR FIVE MINUTES.

THAT'S BETTER.

WHAT DOES GRASS TASTE LIKE ANYWAY?

LIKE BUTTERED MOCHA ALMOND FUDGE ICE CREAM, WHAT DO YOU THINK?

I LOVE BUTTERED MOCHA ALMOND FUDGE ICE CREAM, IT'S MY FAVORITE!!

OOOOKAY, ONLY KIDDING, FREAKO.

AHMM

13

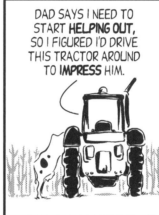

THANK YOU, THAT **CUD'S** BEEN IN THERE FOR A **WEEK**.

CAN I BE DONE NOW?

HAPPY VALENTINE'S DAY. I **GLOB** YOU?

NO, I **HEART** YOU. SEE, THERE'S THE **TWO CHAMBERS**, AND HERE'S THE **AORTIC VALVE**.

I LOOKED IT UP, AND **REAL HEARTS** LOOK NOTHING LIKE THE ONES THEY PUT ON **GREETING CARDS**. I WANTED ACCURACY.

I WAS LESS QUEASY WHEN I THOUGHT YOU **GLOBBED** ME.

SINCE MOM ENROLLED ME IN **SCHOOL** I THOUGHT YOU MIGHT BE FEELING A LITTLE **LONELY**, SO I GOT YOU...

...THIS.

A KITTY?

WIDDLE, IDDEEE, BIDDY!

OK, SO THIS WAS MAYBE A BAD IDEA.

LIKE KOO **HOLD 'EM** IN MA **MOOFF**.

25

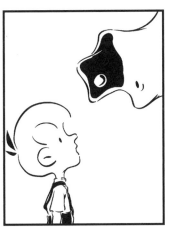

A, A, X, TRIGGER, X, O, B, B, UP, DOWN, UP, DOWN, RIGHT, LEFT, A, A.

BLEEP, BLOOP

HA! THAT **COMBO** JUST **AERIAL PILE-DRIVERED** YOUR FACE INTO **OBLIVION**.

IT HURTS, I KNOW.

CLICKA CLACKA

A, A, X, R, Q TRIGGER, UP, DOWN, SIDE, SIDE, TOGGLE, BACK AND **RED BUTTON!!**

CRACKA!! CRACKLE! CRACK!!

THESE JUST WEREN'T BUILT FOR ME.

YA THINK?

PIZZA-ROLL-**HENGE**.

"CHOMP"

MMMMMMM, MYSTERIOUS AND DELICIOUS.

DO YOU BELIEVE IN THE THEORY OF **TANGENTIAL UNIVERSES**?

LIKE FOR EVERY DECISION YOU MAKE THERE IS A **TANGENT UNIVERSE** WHERE YOU MADE THE **OPPOSITE CHOICE**.

SO THERE IS AN ALTERNATE UNIVERSE THAT EXISTS WHERE YOU DECIDED **NOT** TO BRING UP THE SUBJECT OF TANGENTIAL UNIVERSES?

YUP.

OH, TO BE **THAT** TANGENTIAL COW.

I BET YOU SHE'S NICER THAN YOU.

51

I **SO** NEED MY OWN BATHROOM

I AM MAN OF A BILLION FACES!

AMERICA HAS NOT LOST ITS COMPETITIVE EDGE!! ARE YOU NUTS?!

YOU CAN'T DENY THE GROWTH OF CHINA AND INDIA'S BURGEONING ECONOMIES!!

YEAH, TALK TO ME AGAIN WHEN THEIR PRODUCTIVITY GROWS AT AN ANNUAL 3.5 PERCENT!!

COUNT ON IT!!

GUESS I WON'T BE SHARING ANY MORE OF MY 'TIME' MAGAZINE.

USA HAS SUPERIOR INNOVATION!!

INNOVATE THIS!!

YOU CAN'T KEEP THINGS BOTTLED UP. TELL ME WHAT'S WRONG.

NOTHIN'.

SOMETIMES IT'S JUST BETTER TO TELL ANOTHER PERSON AND MAYBE YOU'LL FIND OUT YOUR PROBLEM IS NOT AS BAD AS YOU'RE MAKING IT OUT TO BE.

OH, OK.

I'M REALLY WORRIED ABOUT MY **TRANS FAT** INTAKE. THERE, I SAID IT. WOW, YOU'RE RIGHT, COW, I DO FEEL BETTER. I GUESS IT WAS SILLY TO WORRY ABOUT SOME **FOOD ADDITIVE.**

NO, **TRANS FATS** ARE PRETTY HORRIBLE. I HEARD YOU MIGHT AS WELL BE DOWNING **PLASTIC EXPLOSIVES**, AS BAD AS THEY ARE FOR YOU. I'D WORRY.

I KNEW IT!!

WHAT'S THE MATTER?

I DON'T KNOW WHAT TO GET MOM FOR MOTHER'S DAY.

I'M SURE SHE'S HAPPY JUST KNOWING YOU **LOVE** AND **APPRECIATE** HER.

REALLY?

AND THE **PERFECT GIFT** WILL LET HER KNOW JUST THAT.

ARE YOU **TORTURING** ME?

IF YOU WERE MY MOM, WHAT WOULD YOU WANT FOR **MOTHER'S DAY?**

WHAT PART OF THE WORD **MIGRAINE** DO YOU **NOT** UNDERSTAND?

BUT I WANNA GO TO **CHUNKY CHEEZY** PIZZA.

SO TAKE YERSELF TO STINKIN' **CHUNKY CHEEZY!!!** I'M **RUNNING** AWAY!!!

FORGET IT! I'M NOT TELLING YOU. YOU'LL JUST **STEAL** MY IDEA LIKE YOU DID LAST YEAR.

I **PROMISE** I WON'T. PLEASE TELL ME WHAT YOU'RE GETTING MOM FOR **MOTHER'S DAY!**

FINE!

WHY AM I **SO** PREDICTABLE?

SHE TOLD YOU SHE WAS **REPAINTING** YOUR MOM'S CAR?

COW, CHECK OUT THE **MOTHER'S DAY** POEM I WROTE FOR MOM.

THE WORD **MOM** MEANS SO MUCH TO SO MANY **KIDS.** BUT IF YOU KNEW WHAT THE LETTERS REALLY MEANT YOU'D FLIP YOUR **LIDS.**

LIDS?

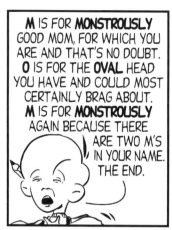
M IS FOR **MONSTROUSLY** GOOD MOM, FOR WHICH YOU ARE AND THAT'S NO DOUBT. **O** IS FOR THE **OVAL** HEAD YOU HAVE AND COULD MOST CERTAINLY BRAG ABOUT. **M** IS FOR **MONSTROUSLY** AGAIN BECAUSE THERE ARE TWO M'S IN YOUR NAME. THE END.

YOU REALLY LIKE THE WORD **MONSTROUSLY.**

ISN'T IT A SWEET WORD?

WRRRR

SUPA-VAC

R
B
C A

AFTER HOURS OF **COVERT** SURVEILLANCE, I'VE DECIDED TO BUY MOM A **BUTLER** FOR MOTHER'S DAY.

YOU HID IN **GARBAGE** AGAIN?

I'VE PRICED IT AND I CAN'T AFFORD TO BUY MOM A **REAL** BUTLER FOR MOTHER'S DAY, SO I'M MAKING **COUPONS** THAT SHE CAN REDEEM TO HAVE **ME** CLEAN THE HOUSE.

FREE SWEEP FLOOR
LOVE, BILLY
FREE VACUUM
WILL NOT FIGHT TRACY

THESE ALL EXPIRE AT **NOON** ON SUNDAY.

I'LL POINT THAT OUT **AFTER** THE FACT.

Cow & Boy present *A Mother's Day Breakfast*

MY SCIENCE PROJECT **WAS** GOING TO FOCUS ON MY INVENTION OF **TELEPORTATION.** BUT THE MORE RESEARCH I DID, THE MORE I DISCOVERED THAT INVENTING TELEPORTATION MAY IN FACT **NOT** BE A GOOD THING.

MY SCIENCE PROJECT:
An Exercise In Restraint

OBSERVE THE FIRST PROBLEM OF TELEPORTATION AS SHOWN IN THIS **PHOTOSHOP RENDERING.**

Exhibit **A:**

HERE YOU SEE THE RESULT OF USING THE TELEPORTATION MACHINE AT THE SAME TIME AS A FRIEND. CHANCES ARE YOUR MOLECULES WILL **INTERTWINE,** ENDING UP WITH AN OUTCOME NOT UNLIKE THIS.

NOW LET'S CHECK OUT **EXHIBIT B.**

EXHIBIT B:

Exhibit **A:**

EVEN IF YOU USE THE TELEPORTATION POD ALONE, WHAT ARE THE CHANCES THAT **TRILLIONS** OF MOLECULES THAT HAVE BEEN BLOWN APART WILL BE **REASSEMBLED** IN THE EXACT SAME SPOT? THE ODDS AREN'T GOOD.

Exhibit

I'D HAVE TO SAY UNLESS WE WANT A WORLD OF HALF-HUMAN, HALF-ANIMAL **MUTANTS** WITH ARMS COMING OUT OF THEIR FOREHEADS, TELEPORTATION IS BETTER LEFT **UNINVENTED.**

In Conclusion:
Mankind better off without it.

YOU TOLD ME YOU WERE DOING PHOTO-SYNTHESIS.

MY PLANT DIED.

In Conclusion:
Mankind better off without it.

+2
ANYONE?

LEARN

IT SAYS HERE THAT THE U.S. POPULATION WILL SOON REACH **300 MILLION.**

WOW, I WONDER WHAT YOU GET FOR BEING THE **300 MILLIONTH** U.S. CITIZEN.

OOH, MAYBE IT'S A **GEORGE FOREMAN GRILL.** MAN, WOULDN'T IT STINK TO BE NUMBER **299,999,999?**

YOU'D BE LIKE, "HEY, I'M 299,999,999. GIVE ME MY FOREMAN GRILL." THEY'D BE LIKE, **"NEXT!"** WOW, THAT'D BE **HARSH.**

WHY DO **YOU** WANT A GRILL?

COW, YOUR **PRESCRIPTION** TO 'CELEB-STAR GAZER' HAS ARRIVED.

CELEB ☆ GAZER!
J.Lo Wants thing!
HOT HOLLYWOOD

YOU MEAN **SUBSCRIPTION.** YOU SAID **PRESCRIPTION.** A DOCTOR **PRE**SCRIBES DRUGS BUT ONE **SUB**SCRIBES TO A MAGAZINE.

OF COURSE I DO **NEED** MY 'CELEB-STAR GAZER' MAGAZINE **LIKE** A DRUG. SO MAYBE **PRESCRIPTION** IS NOT THAT FAR OFF. HMMMMM....

TAP, TAP

OH, JUST GIVE IT HERE, WILL YA?!!

YEAH, I'M NOT SO SURE.

HOW CAN YOU READ THAT **CRUD?!**

GOT JUICE?
CELEB ☆ GAZER
J. Lo Wants Something!

WHY DO YOU WANT TO READ ABOUT WHAT SOME **FAMOUS SO-AND-SO** HAD TO DRINK AT **STARBUCKS** LAST THURSDAY?

I FIND IT REASSURING TO KNOW THAT NO MATTER HOW FAMOUS A STAR GETS, HE OR SHE CAN ENJOY THEIR COFFEE IN DRESS-DOWN SWEATS AND ARE JUST AS HUMAN AS YOU OR ME.

YOU'RE A COW.

DON'T RUIN THIS FOR ME.

DO YOU THINK THE U.S. HAS ABUSED ITS SOLE **SUPER-POWER** STATUS AROUND THE WORLD SINCE THE END OF **THE COLD WAR?**

THE COLD WAR BEING WHEN THE U.S. SWIFTLY BEAT **SANTA CLAUS** AND HIS **ELVISH NORTH POLE ALLIANCE** FOR CONTROL OF THE TERRITORY WE NOW CALL **ALASKA?**

IF YOU KNOW OF ANOTHER **COLD** WAR, I'M ALL EARS.

JUST CHECKING.

IS THAT **MY** FISH BOWL?

THE GYPSY IS IN

IT'S MY **CRYSTAL BALL** AND IT TELLS ME YOUR GOLDFISH IS ENJOYING HIS NEW ACCOMMODATIONS IN A BUCKET NEXT TO THE GARAGE.

I AM A **GYPSY** AND FOR THE PRICE OF A **LITTLE DEBBIE** SNACK CAKE I WILL LOOK INTO MY CRYSTAL BALL AND REVEAL TO YOU YOUR FUTURE.

BIT OF AN OVER-ELABORATE WAY TO SCORE A LITTLE DEBBIE, DON'T YOU THINK?

PERHAPS, IF THEY WEREN'T SO WICKED DELICIOUS.

THE GYPSY IS IN

I SEE A FUTURE FILLED WITH DISAPPOINTMENT.

A FUTURE OF QUIET DESPERATION, WITH ONE FALSE HOPE AFTER ANOTHER.

YUP, FAILURE COMPOUNDING UPON MORE FAILURE... AT LEAST THROUGH MOST OF THIS AFTERNOON.

I TOLD YOU FISHING IS NOT ABOUT **CATCHING** THE FISH.

CRYSTAL BALL KNOWS YOU'RE LYING.

THE GYPSY IS IN

84

I'VE DECIDED IT MIGHT BE A GOOD IDEA IF WE START SAVING FOR **RETIREMENT.**

IT'S IMPORTANT WE ARE PROVIDED FOR LATER IN LIFE. NOW THE AVERAGE SAVINGS FOR SOMEONE RETIRING TODAY IN THE U.S. IS ABOUT $600,000.

TAP, TAP

IF I FACTOR IN A LITTLE INFLATION BASED ON CURRENT TRENDS, GAS PRICES, HOUSING COSTS, ETC. I CAN DETERMINE THE **EXACT** AMOUNT WE'LL NEED WHEN WE RETIRE.

$12.7 BILLION.

HMM, **LESS** THAN I THOUGHT.

AHHHH, MY LEG!!

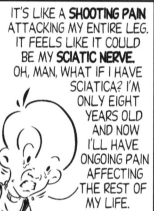

IT'S LIKE A **SHOOTING PAIN** ATTACKING MY ENTIRE LEG. IT FEELS LIKE IT COULD BE MY **SCIATIC NERVE.** OH, MAN, WHAT IF I HAVE SCIATICA? I'M ONLY EIGHT YEARS OLD AND NOW I'LL HAVE ONGOING PAIN AFFECTING THE REST OF MY LIFE.

THIS ISN'T FAIR!! WHY IS THIS HAPPENING TO ME?! WHY?!! WHYYY?!!

OH, WAIT! IT'S ONLY A **PITCHFORK.**

YEOW, THAT'S IN THERE DEEP.

ISN'T IT FUNNY HOW **MONEY** CORRUPTS AND RUINS EVERYTHING THAT'S **GOOD AND PURE?**

HEE, TEE, HEE...

HA, HA, HA HA, HA, HA, HA.

NO, NOT FUNNY HA-HA.

OH... RIGHT.

I'VE SET UP THIS **VIDEO CAMERA** IN THE FOREST SO WE CAN CATCH **BIGFOOT** ON TAPE.

I FIGURE IT'S ONLY A MATTER OF TIME BEFORE THE **MIGHTY BEAST** PASSES IN FRONT OF THE CAMERA, AND THEN WE CAN SELL THE FOOTAGE FOR **MILLIONS**.

AND BY **MATTER OF TIME** YOU MEAN **NEVER**, RIGHT?

HEY, I'VE BEEN OUT HERE **FIVE HOURS** ALREADY AND I'LL WAIT AS LONG AS...

...WHOOPS, FORGOT THE TAPE.

LET ME KNOW HOW ALL THIS PANS OUT.

CHECK OUT MY **BIGFOOT** COSTUME. I MADE IT FROM MY OLD **PAJAMAS** AND SOME DISCARDED **HAIR CLIPPINGS** FROM THE BARBER SHOP.

I GOT TIRED OF WAITING FOR BIGFOOT TO SHOW UP SO I FIGURE I'LL JUST FILM SOMEONE WEARING THIS INSTEAD.

SOMEONE'S ACTUALLY GOING TO **WEAR** THAT?

YES, BUT YOU CAN'T, YOU'RE A **QUADRUPED**. THE PUBLIC WOULD NEVER BUY IT. AND I OF COURSE CAN'T WEAR IT BECAUSE I NEED TO **DIRECT** THE FOOTAGE.

WHO THEN?

SO WHAT'S THE BIG HURRY THAT I HAVE TO SKIP 'MACGYVER' FOR?

I GIVE YOU BIGFOOT.

DID WE HAVE TO **SUPER-GLUE** THE HAIR DIRECTLY TO MY FACE?

SORRY, MARTIN, BUT THE CAMERA WON'T LIE. WE NEED **AUTHENTICITY** IF WE'RE GOING TO GET THE WORLD TO BELIEVE YOU'RE **BIGFOOT**.

DOES BIGFOOT WEAR GLASSES?

GOOD POINT, COW. BETTER GIVE ME THESE, MARTIN.

BUT I CAN'T **SEE** WITHOUT MY GLASSES.

PLEASE, MARTIN, WE NEED BIGFOOT TO LOOK **REAL**.

I'M THREE FOOT TWO!

THERE I WAS, **SAWING** OFF NARWHAL HORN AFTER NARWHAL HORN. IT WAS LIKE THE WEIRDEST **DREAM** EVER.

POOR NAR-WHALS.

TELL ME ABOUT IT. BUT YOU HAVEN'T HEARD THE WEIRDEST PART. WHEN I WOKE UP I WAS IN THE UPSTAIRS HALLWAY HOLDING A **JIGSAW.**

NO WAY.

I'VE LEARNED THAT NO MATTER WHAT I DO I'M NEVER GOING TO MAKE **EVERYONE** HAPPY.

I MAY MAKE A **FEW** PEOPLE HAPPY HERE AND THERE ALONG THE WAY.

BUT THERE ARE **SOME** PEOPLE WHOM YOU JUST **CAN'T** PLEASE.

AND YOU KNOW WHAT? I AM OK WITH THAT.

WOW, THAT'S VERY BIG OF YOU, BILLY.

YOUR MOM STILL MAD YOU SOLD HER **PORCELAIN GNOME COLLECTION** ON EBAY?

YET, SOMEONE ELSE OUT THERE IS QUITE HAPPY.

SOCRATES ONCE SAID THAT THE **UNEXAMINED LIFE** IS NOT WORTH LIVING.

WHO ARE ALL THOSE PEOPLE?

I DON'T KNOW, BUT IT'S STARTING TO CREEP ME OUT.

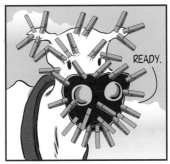

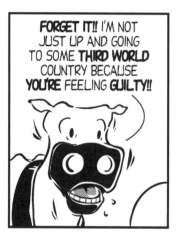

"WOW, COW, HERE WE ARE AT THE **STATE FAIR.** WILL YOU JUST TAKE IT ALL IN? THE SIGHTS. THE SMELLS."

THEY HAVE GOT JUST ABOUT ANY BIT OF FRIED FOOD ON A STICK YOU COULD EVER WANT.

SNIFF

BUT WE MUST BE STRONG. YOU HAVE A COMPETITION TO WIN, AND IF WE...**HEY**... IS IT **RAINING?**

CHURROS. AGGHHH.

SICK!

WOW, **FRIED-CHOCOLATE-PICKLE-ON-A-STICK,** AND IT'S DELICIOUS. I LOVE **THE FAIR.**

BETTER GO TO THE STABLE AND CHECK ON COW. SHE LOOKED A LITTLE NERVOUS ABOUT THE COMPETITION.

YOU DIDN'T.

...EAT...
...WHEN...
...NERVOUS...
YOU KNOW THIS.

WHAT ARE YOU DOING?

I'M SPENDING THE NIGHT OUT HERE WITH YOU IN THE **STABLE.**

WHY?

SOMETIMES PEOPLE TRY TO **SABOTAGE** THE COWS THE NIGHT BEFORE A BIG COMPETITION. I WANT TO PROTECT YOU, COW.

WOW, BILLY, THANKS.

YER OUT HERE SO I WON'T RAID THE **FRIED-CHOCOLATE-PICKLE-ON-A-STICK** TENT. AND THERE'S THAT.

EVER HAVE ONE OF THOSE DAYS WHEN YOU JUST WAKE UP HAPPY AND **NOTHING** CAN BRING YOU DOWN?

NOT EVEN **STARVING CHILDREN** IN THE POOR, DISHEVELED PLACES OF THE WORLD?

NOPE.

WHAT ABOUT THE CLIMATE-CHANGING **OZONE HOLE?**

OZONE SHMOZONE.

REMEMBER THE SEASON FINALE OF **THE OC?**

MARISSA!! WHY?!!!

CHECK IT, COW! I MADE US SOME **LUNCH.**

A LITTLE PEANUT BUTTER AND JELLY ACTION.

THEY'RE NOT BABY TRIANGLES!!!

NOW MAYBE NEXT TIME YOU'LL REMEMBER.

NEXT TIME?

OK, DRACULA, WEREWOLF AND FRANKENSTEIN IN A **STEEL CAGE** MATCH, WHO WINS?

GAMERA, HANDS DOWN.

A GIANT, RADIOACTIVE FLYING TURTLE WASN'T ONE OF THE CHOICES.

OH, WASN'T HE?

Y'SEE GAMERA HEARD ABOUT YOUR LITTLE STEEL CAGE MATCH BEING ADVERTISED ON HIS FAVORITE MORNING RADIO SHOW. HE THEN TOOK IT UPON HIMSELF TO SWOOP IN AND CRASH THE PARTY.

WHY CAN'T YOU EVER JUST **ANSWER** A QUESTION?

GAMERA SHOOTS LASERS. PYOW, PYOW!!

107

YOU KNOW THERE HAVE BEEN LIKE OVER **1,000** DOCUMENTED **WARS** THROUGHOUT MAN'S HISTORY.

OH, WHAT ARE YOU COMPLAINING ABOUT? A LITTLE WAR NEVER KILLED ANYBODY.

SCRATCH WHAT I SAID JUST THEN.

ALREADY DID.

WHATEVER HAPPENED TO **"THE WALTONS"**?

WHO?

YOU KNOW, GOOD FAMILY TV SHOWS. IT SEEMS LIKE HALF THE SHOWS ON TV TODAY ARE EITHER ABOUT PROFILING **SERIAL KILLERS** OR **CRIME SCENE INVESTIGATION.**

AND TO MAKE IT WORSE, WHEN ONE OF THOSE SHOWS IS SUCCESSFUL, **SPINOFF** SHOWS ARE CREATED JUST TO QUENCH THE PUBLIC'S **INSATIABLE** THIRST FOR THE **GROTESQUE.** WHAT'S WITH AMERICA'S **MORBID** FASCINATION WITH THE **SICK** AND....

COOL!

DUDE! WHAT **WAS** THIS?

YOU EVER NOTICE HOW PEOPLE DON'T SAY THEY'RE **SORRY** ANYMORE?

PEOPLE WILL ARGUE, ARGUE, ARGUE UNTIL THEY ARE BLUE IN THE FACE, BUT THEY WILL NEVER ADMIT TO ANY WRONGDOING.

I PERSONALLY THINK IT TAKES MORE **CHARACTER** TO JUST SAY YOU'RE SORRY.

I'M NOT APOLOGIZING FOR AN ACCIDENT.

YOU CUT THE BUTT OUT OF MY OVERALLS!!

CORRECTION. I **ACCIDENTALLY** CUT THE BUTT OUT OF YOUR OVERALLS.

THE FIRST LEAF OF FALL.

ANOTHER SUMMER OF MY YOUTH HAS PASSED ME BY.

SOMEHOW I KNEW THOSE CAREFREE DAYS WOULD COME TO AN END.

THIS LEAF IS JUST NATURE'S WAY OF SAYING, "THE PARTY'S OVER. IT'S TIME TO PAY THE BILL."

FWIT

PLOP

THAT WAS AN $80 ROD.

HEFTY BILL.

MOM, YOU'VE GOT TO TAKE ME BACK TO THE MALL AND BUY ME SOME MORE SCHOOL CLOTHES!!

ONE KID PUSHED ME OVER AND MOCKED INTEREST IN MY OVERALLS, AND THEN A LITTLE GIRL SNICKERED. SHE SNICKERED, MOM!!

WOW, THAT'S HORRIBLE.

MAYBE YOU SHOULDN'T HAVE GIVEN ALL YOUR NEW CLOTHES AWAY. I CAN'T AFFORD TO BUY YOU ANY MORE.

NO, THIS CAN'T BE HAPPENING.

WHY'RE YOU CUTTING YOUR OVERALLS IN HALF?

SO THE WORLD WILL LOVE ME!!

THAT'S YOUR MOM'S CREDIT CARD.

I KNOW.

MASTERCHARGE

NO DEPARTMENT STORE WILL EVER LET YOU USE IT TO BUY NEW SCHOOL CLOTHES. WHY ARE YOU LOOKING AT ME LIKE THAT?

TRENDZ

15% off with card

WELL, HERE I AM. IT'S THE **SECOND DAY** OF SCHOOL.

AND EVEN THOUGH TRENDY CLOTHES GO AGAINST WHO I AM, I REALIZE THAT IF I PRESENT MYSELF IN A WAY THAT IS MORE COMFORTING TO MY PEERS, THEY MIGHT LET THEIR GUARD DOWN AND GET TO KNOW ME.

NICE **VON DUTCH** HAT, **DORKUS AURELIUS!**

AHHHH!!!

POOSH

MORE METAL

OK, SO IT'S JUST A KIND OF INDISCRIMINATING-HATRED-TOWARD-ME-IN-GENERAL THING. **MIGHT HAVE TOLD ME THAT $564.32 AT THE GAP AGO, THANK YOU!**

I'M WRITING A **SCREENPLAY**, COW. IT'S A HORROR MOVIE AND IT'S QUITE POSSIBLY THE SCARIEST COLLECTION OF WORDS EVER PUT TO PAPER.

IT CAME TO ME IN A DREAM. RATHER, I SHOULD SAY A **NIGHTMARE**. THINK OF THE TWO MOST TERRIFYING THINGS EVER. NOW **COMBINE** THEM.

MY SCRIPT IS TITLED... **"TORNADO SHARKS"**

YOUR MOVIE HAS SHARKS BLOWING AROUND IN TORNADOES?

I JUST GOT A CHILL WHEN YOU SAID THAT.

EVERY GOOD MOVIE NEEDS A STELLAR POSTER. CHECK OUT WHAT I ROUGHED UP IN PHOTOSHOP.

TORNADO SHARKS

WHO KNOWS WHAT EVIL LURKS IN THE ?

YOUR TAGLINE IS... "WHO KNOWS WHAT EVIL LURKS IN THE HEARTS OF TORNADOES? SHARKS THAT'S WHAT."

KIND OF ROLLS RIGHT OFF THE TONGUE.

YES, BUT SO DOES DROOL.

I'M STUCK, COW. I CAN'T THINK OF AN ENDING FOR MY SCRIPT FOR "TORNADO SHARKS."

A TORNADO SHARK IS ON THE VERGE OF DESTROYING ALL OF MANKIND BUT THEN HE DISCOVERS HIS INNER CHILD.

ALL GOOD MOVIES DEFY GENRE IN SOME WAY. "TORNADO SHARKS" ISN'T ALL HORROR. IT'S ABOUT HEART, TOO.

MAYBE TORNADO SHARK DISCOVERS HIS INNER CHILD IS JUST ONE HE SWALLOWED ALONG THE WAY.

OOH, A **TWIST** ENDING. I LIKE IT.

WELL, MY SCRIPT'S OFFICIALLY DONE.

Torna Sh Based True

"TORNADO SHARKS" BASED ON A TRUE STORY.

A **TRUE STORY?**

WELL, TORNADOES AND SHARKS BOTH EXIST AND NOBODY CAN PROVE THAT THIS **DIDN'T** HAPPEN.

A TORNADO SHARK TAKES OUT THE EIFFEL TOWER IN THE FIRST ACT.

I DON'T LIKE YOUR TONE.

I WONDER WHO I SHOULD GET TO DIRECT **"TORNADO SHARKS."**

SIGNS

ARMAGEDDON

M. NIGHT SHYAMALAN WILL BE ABLE TO GIVE "TORNADO SHARKS" THE SUBTLE TREATMENT AND LAYERED TEXTURE THAT A STORY LIKE THIS DESERVES.

BUT "TORNADO SHARKS" MIGHT REQUIRE THE ADRENALINE SHOTS OF BOMBASTIC THRILLERY THAT ONLY A **MICHAEL BAY** CAN DELIVER.

I ALWAYS PICTURED "TORNADO SHARKS" AS A **MERCHANT IVORY** PRODUCTION

NOW YOU'RE MAKING FUN.

WELL, IT'S TIME TO CELEBRATE, COW.

I JUST SENT OFF MY SCRIPT, **"TORNADO SHARKS,"** TO EVERY MAJOR HOLLYWOOD STUDIO.

I FIGURE I HAVE ABOUT TWO WEEKS BEFORE IT'S GREEN LIT AND PUT INTO PRODUCTION. THEN THEY'LL BE BEATING DOWN MY DOOR FOR A SEQUEL.

HOW DOES **"TORNADO SHARKS 2: I THINK THINGS JUST GOT A LITTLE MORE WINDY,"** SOUND?

SCARY?

AFTER COLLEGE I THINK I'M GOING TO TAKE A YEAR OFF AND BACKPACK THROUGH EUROPE.

I WANT TO GET TO KNOW THE WORLD.

I'LL ONLY STAY IN HOSTELS AND EAT WHAT I CAN SCROUNGE OR WHAT OTHERS OFFER. I'LL TAKE MY TIME AND LEARN HOW DIFFERENT CULTURES LIVE AND RELATE TO ONE ANOTHER. I WILL GAIN A NEW PERSPECTIVE ON LIFE AND FORM A SET OF IDEALS ON WHICH TO LIVE MY OWN LIFE.

EVENTUALLY MY TRAVELS WILL TAKE ME BACK HOME. OVER TIME I'LL GET A JOB, GET MARRIED, HAVE 2.5 KIDS, GET A MORTGAGE AND TWO SUV'S, AND SLOWLY FORGET WHATEVER IDEALS I PICKED UP IN EUROPE. I'LL PANIC TO MYSELF OFF AND ON FOR ABOUT 10 YEARS, AND THEN ULTIMATELY FIND SOME LEVEL OF HAPPINESS KNOWING I PROBABLY HAD NO REAL CHOICE IN ANYTHING ANYWAY.

WELL, SEND ME A POSTCARD.

I WILL.

I CAN'T WAIT 'TIL I GROW UP TO BE JUST LIKE YOU, DAD.

I JUST HOPE I HAVE MORE HAIR.

DON'T WORRY, YOU WON'T.

DO YOU THINK GOD IS MORE AN ARTIST OR AN ENGINEER?

LIKE, IS SPACE HIS CANVAS AND DOES HE HAVE SOME KIND OF GIANT PAINT PALETTE FILLED WITH DIFFERENT ATOMIC ELEMENTS AND PRIMORDIAL GOO WHICH HE MIXES IN DIFFERENT WAYS TO COMPOSE THE UNIVERSE?

OR DOES GOD SIT DOWN AT SOME DRAFTING TABLE METICULOUSLY PORING OVER DESIGNS AND EQUATIONS SO THAT EVERYTHING IN THE WORLD FITS JUST RIGHT?

I DON'T KNOW. BUT I BET HE USES HIS BEARD HAIR FOR HIS GIANT BRUSHES.

WHY DOES A HOUSE THAT COSTS $50,000 IN 1970 COST $200,000 TODAY? WHY CAN'T SOMETHING BE WORTH WHAT IT ALWAYS WAS?

WELL, THERE ARE SHIFTS IN SUPPLY AND DEMAND, AND GLOBAL MARKETS ARE ALSO BROUGHT INTO PLAY.

EXCHANGE RATES PLAY PICKLE WITH CURRENCIES. MORE PEOPLE COMPETE FOR THE SAME JOBS AND ALL OF THIS INFO IS FED INTO THE GREENSPANATRON 5000.

WHICH SPITS OUT A BUNCH OF NUMBERY EQUATIONS ABOUT MONEY AND JUNK 'N' STUFF.

YOU HAVE NO IDEA WHAT YOU'RE SAYING.